Jackinah Denise, "THE" Strong Willed Survivor Presents:

THERE IS

Beauty

BEYOND THE SCARS

PROCLAIMING WHOLENESS BEYOND
THE BLEMISHES OF CANCER

Jackinah Denise

& 9 Courageous Women Declaring That
They Are Strong Willed Survivors

THERE IS BEAUTY BEYOND THE SCARS

All rights reserved. No part of this book may be reproduced, distributed or transmitted in any forms by any means, graphic, electronic, or mechanical, including photocopy, recording, taping, or by any information storage or retrieval system, without permission in writing from the publisher, except in the case of reprints in the context of reviews, quotes or references.

Scripture quotations marked NLT are taken from the Holy Bible, New Living Translation Copyright © 1996, 2004, 2007, 2013, 2015 by Tyndale House Publishers Inc. Scripture quotations marked KJV are taken from the King James Version, Public domain. Scripture quotations marked MSG are taken from The Message Bible, Copyright © 1993, 1994, 1995, 1995, 1996, 2000, 2001, 2002 by Eugene H. Peterson. Scripture quotations are taken from The Holy Bible, New International Version® NIV® Copyright © 1973, 1978, 1984, 2011 by Biblica, Inc.™

Used by permission. All rights reserved worldwide

Copyright © 2023 Jackinah Denise

ISBN: 979-8-9868570-3-9

Printed in the United States of America

For pricing, shipping, information on Visionary Author, book tour, and speaking engagements email: info@beyondthescars.org or visit: www.beyondthescars.org

For my Grammy (my butterfly) and Mama (my angel on earth) who gave me my foundation in Christ and taught me to always believe in myself…

For my parents who gave me life and raised me; Wendal LaVette (lung cancer and coronary artery disease survivor), Karen Denise (28-year cancer survivor and survivor of LIFE), James Brown (my butterfly) and T.Henry (my butterfly)…

For JaNeal and Michael, my two sons and my heartbeats, who have walked this eight year journey with me as my sole caregivers, my medical power of attorney, my biggest supporters and encouragers. Without you two there is no me and the love and appreciation I have for you both will never end- LNE. Thank you for all your many sacrifices so I can continue to live…

For Jaymes and Jaren and my three beautiful nieces; Gia, Zennia, and Zena, my sisters-in-love Roni and Tish, my uncles and aunts (cancer survivors and butterflies), the love ones who did not make it to see their 38th birthday and my extended family members. Words cannot express how much your love, support, and encouragement has meant to me…

For every Bishop, Pastor, Elder, Church Mother, First Lady, Prayer Warrior and Friend who has prayed with me and for me even when I didn't have the strength to pray for myself…

*For every person who could not **see my beauty beyond the scars,** but through them I've learned there is no love like self-love…*

For the men, women, and children who have heard those three devastating words, "YOU HAVE cancer," and those who love us; caregivers, support systems, extended family members and friends...

For those who will be diagnosed with a chronic illness in the future and for the butterflies (including; my Strong Willed Sister and Brother Marvina, Trina, and Marc) who have deposited so many pearls of wisdom and trusted us to carry the torch...and For the families and friends of each co-author (including their butterflies)...

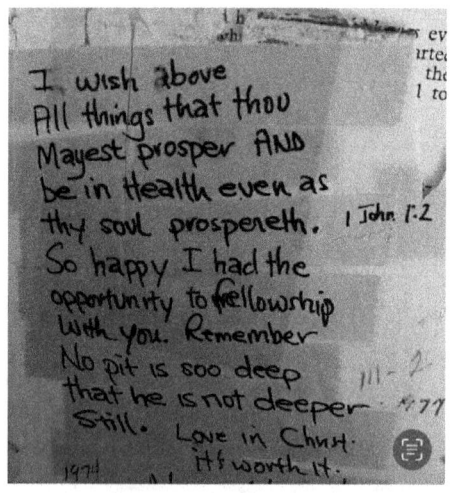

Words of Daisy LaVette

FOREWORD

I remember the first conversation I had with Jackinah Denise, who many affectionately call Kina. It amazed me how someone who had experienced a plethora of trauma, suffering, and hurt never stopped climbing her mountain of faith, hope, and purpose. She did not hold back in her thoughts or emotions the first time we talked. I remember her sharing with me the details of her procedures from prep to recovery. How she had to balance being a single mother and at times painful side effects and reactions to medications, as well as the mental toll the amputation of both breasts has caused her.

Over seven years, Kina has endured a journey of pain and patience, struggle and strength, and fear and faith. What do you do when everything you know to be normal in your life turns upside down in a matter of minutes? What do you do when divorce is in front of you and memories of what you once delighted in are behind you? What do you do when you have so much to live for, but you feel time could be running out?

I remember reading a recent post from Kina that said, "I isolated myself. I thought, how could someone love me with all these scars when I didn't even like to look at myself in the mirror or cried while in the shower?" She goes on to say, "I didn't know that I could get to a place in my life where I could truly love ME until God took me on this process of seeing The Beauty Beyond the Scars." Wow, what a testament of faith giving God permission to lead even while you are bleeding. What a testament of trust that even in the constant reminder of our scars, there is a love in Christ so deep that surpasses our understanding.

Kina's walk is one of strength and hope. Therefore, this book reflects that. Kina, along with nine other co-authors who are cancer survivors and caregivers made a choice to see the beauty beyond the scars. It's not easy to look at a scar. I look at one daily on my left hand that came from an accident in college. I remember the incident as if it happened yesterday. I remember the tears I cried and the days and months I had to nurse a second-degree burn. Scars are constant reminders of the rain but seeing beyond the scars is where you can appreciate the rainbow. I remember when I had a chance to speak to the group of writers for this book. I presented a workshop entitled, Be the Author of Your Joy Story, I told them that this book is a masterpiece, which means a work of outstanding artistry, skill, or workmanship.

Because of the depth of their pain, you will feel the authenticity of each author's story and envelop their cloak of wisdom and courage. In this book, you will find hope and healing. In this book, you will also find the power of love and forgiveness. Pema Chodren said, "The greatest obstacle to connecting to your joy is resentment." You can not be skilled in your workmanship if you are bitter, resentful, and unforgiving. What I love about this book is that Kina, along with the other co-authors are not only transparent about their pain, but also their purpose. Whenever you come into your purpose in Christ, you have tapped into unlimited power!

The tenacity of these women reminds me of the beautiful Alice Walker. Born in 1944, the eighth child of African American sharecroppers. She was accidentally blinded in one eye, so her mother gave her a typewriter, allowing her to write instead of doing chores. After graduating (1965) from Sarah Lawrence College, Walker moved to Mississippi and began teaching and publishing her works. She had every reason to give up, to resent what happened to her but instead she turned a painful situation into her greatest momentum. Because of that, we have books such as The Color Purple, In Love & Trouble, Possessing the Secret of Joy, and countless others.

Kina is an advocate that will fight until her last breath to share her story and stand for other women who are too weak, fragile, and afraid to stand for themselves. She wants you to know that you are not in this alone. Join Kina, along with the other co-authors on this journey we call life. This is not a book of self-pity but of self-worth. Your scars may look like there is no hope, but it's beyond the scars where the abundance of fullness, fulfillment, and fragrance resides.

Min. Carenda Deonne Beamon – M.A. in Law

Author/Speaker/Certified Stress Management Coach

ACKNOWLEDGEMENTS

I AM THANKFUL, GRATEFUL, AND BLESSED!

I AM THANKFUL…

That God didn't give up on me and didn't allow me to give up on myself.
Thankfully, through all of life's curveballs, even bruised and scarred, I'm able to leap over walls, show unconditional love and begin walking in my God-given PURPOSE to EDUCATE, ADVOCATE and CELEBRATE LIFE!

I AM GRATEFUL…

For all the encounters (positive and negative) that have taught me how to SEE THE BEAUTY BEYOND THE SCARS of not just cancer, but of life.

For the experiences of life that helped me understand my mom's journey which ultimately led to us having a strong mother-daughter relationship.

Charlene Cotti, my "Mama-Boober"
Melanie Brown
Ashley Dennis
Strong Willed Survivor Beyond The Scars Team
Beyond Boobs/ Flat Out Love (cancer support groups)
TYFBF & STB Sponsors; Jason Charles w/ Jay's Creations, MEEC Luxury Ventures,
Ernest Smith and The Makeup School by Sarah Rillon

I AM BLESSED...

To have some amazing people in my life who recognized the greatness inside of me and encouraged me to become the child of God, mother, daughter, sister, fun-loving aunt, friend, and Visionary Author I was created to be.

My Big Sister in Christ, Carmen Anthony
My Life Coach, Min. Carenda Deonne Beamon
Pastor Floyd and Mother Linda Hawkins
Bishop K.W. Brown, Elder Valery Brown and my Mount Global Fellowship of Churches family
Bishop G. Wesley Hardy, First Lady Doris Hardy and my Cathedral of Faith C.O.G.I.C family
My Project Manager, Ifedayo Greenway

Contents

FOREWORD v

ACKNOWLEDGEMENTS ix

INTRODUCTION 1

THE INVITATION
Lauren Wingrove *(Cancer Survivor)* 3

PERSPECTIVE IS IMPORTANT
Mary A. *(Cancer Survivor/Caregiver)* 5

UNTIL IT'S DIFFERENT
Erica "Lala" Morgan *(Cancer Survivor)* 18

RESILIENCE
Leonetta Jules & Taneja Jules *(Caregiver/ Childhood Cancer Survivor)* 25

SHE CALLED ME ANGEL FACE 34
Amber Curtis *(Daughter of a Butterfly)* 34

THE SUNDAY BEFORE 11.24.19.21.36
Michelle Wicker & Jordynne Wicker
(Caregiver/Granddaughter of a Butterfly) 38

11.24.19.21.36
Jordynne Wicker 43

SHE PERSISTED
Melody Hansley *(Daughter of a Butterfly)*........................48

I WAS GIVEN THESE MOUNTAINS
Jackinah Denise *(Cancer Survivor/Caregiver/Daughter of a Butterfly)*........................57

WHAT MAKES YOU A STRONG WILLED SURVIVOR
Lauren Wingrove........................79

JOURNAL NOTES 81

DISCLAIMER: 82

ABOUT THE AUTHORS 83

INTRODUCTION

"Now faith is confidence in what we hope for and assurance about what we do not see (Hebrews 11:1)."

Approximately 39.6% of men and women will be diagnosed with cancer at some point during their lifetime and in 2014, the year I was originally diagnosed there were approximately 2.85 million children in the United States living with at least one parent battling or surviving some type of cancer.

Whether you are a person diagnosed with cancer, know someone who has been diagnosed, or a caregiver caring for a loved one, breast, colon, prostate, stomach, thyroid, lung, kidney, liver, lymphoma, and the many (numerous) other types of cancers, this horrible disease impacts our entire community. Yes, it is a worldwide major health problem impacting children, teens, young adults, and even those over the age of 40.

This project is a collection of testimonies from some of the strongest people with some of the toughest battles. A total of 10 women; Lauren, Mary, Erica, Leonetta, Taneja, Amber, Michelle, Jordynne, Melody, and me, Jackinah Denise "THE" Strong Willed Survivor, striving to see the beauty beyond the scars left from the impact of cancer, all varying in age, from different backgrounds; cancer patients, survivors, caregivers, and family members of butterflies (those no longer physically with us).

It is a proven fact that people gain more courage, strength, and knowledge by coming in direct contact with others who have experienced similar situations.

Even though not all of the numerous types of cancers are listed on these pages a few of them are and it is our prayer that through our vulnerability, sharing the most personal and precious moments of our lives, we will be able to:

- Give a point of view from someone impacted.
- Explain the different diagnoses, side effects, and treatments.
- Help someone understand the emotional roller coaster being diagnosed or having a loved one diagnosed may take you on.
- And ultimately stress the importance of regular check-ups. If something doesn't seem right or feel right, please go get checked. You are your best advocate, and you are worth fighting for.

THE INVITATION

Lauren Wingrove

(Cancer Survivor)

I remember the day
my invitation came
Invisible ink on pink paper
As my tears wet the page
The words were revealed
To say "You have cancer."

I walk to the door
Pink ribbon in hand
A three step dance
And I'm ushered in
To wait my turn
Until the battle begins

So with armor cracked
And my sword unsheathed
Poison infused blade
Plunged in deep
I waged a war
To save myself

Proclaiming Wholeness Beyond The Blemishes Of Cancer

As I grew weak,
my army stayed strong
Hundreds of soldiers marching along
To the cadence of love
Fighting for me
When my wounds cut deep

The ground trembled and shook
With the power of prayer
As thousands of enemies
Fell to their death
Screams muffled under stolen breaths
And the chorus of victory bells

I remember the day
my invitation came
Invisible ink on pink paper
As my tears wet the page
The words were revealed to say
"You beat cancer."

I run my fingers
on the ridges of my scars
lashed across my chest
like a pink scarlet letter

PERSPECTIVE IS IMPORTANT

Mary A.

(Cancer Survivor/Caregiver)

Perspective is important…I would have fainted had I not believed…

It's 2013. I was a single mother to a five-year-old daughter. I was in a relationship for almost four years. My mom lived with me (since my dad passed from metastatic cancer, for which I was a caregiver). I needed a change. I packed up and moved to get a start fresh with my mom and my daughter. After the move, things were great! I was in top shape. I was making friends. My daughter was thriving. Money wasn't as tight, and we were living like tourists. I celebrated my 35th birthday on August 18th. We went on a sailboat excursion, and I introduced my new friends to coconut rum. Shortly after my birthday, I performed a self-exam. I knew 35 was the magic age to schedule my first mammogram because my mom is a breast cancer survivor.

The rule is if you have a family history, you start five years earlier. With two parents having cancer, I knew I had to be vigilant. I step in the shower excited to do what I know to do and make sure I have early detection should this thing decide to hit me too! I'm somewhat excited not to be a statistic. Again, I'm in top shape. This only happens to people who don't take care of themselves. I checked my right breast. Nothing. Check. I checked the left breast and paused. I checked the tip of my left breast again. I slid my fingers down against my skin and paused again. I felt a knot that was the size of a golf ball. I immediately got out of the shower and stood in the mirror. My left breast was hanging lower than my right. I raised my arms. There was a bulge under my left underarm. I thought to myself, *this can't be*. I was in disbelief and didn't want to process what I thought was happening. I left all of my personal doctors and a well-known hospital system to be in this new location where I knew no one. I went to the ER immediately. While there, I was told there was probably nothing to worry about. I'm young. It doesn't look typical. It's not against my breast wall. I don't have any discharge. My nipple isn't inverted. They couldn't do anything at the time but provided me with a new primary Care Physician who should be able to get me more assistance.

I went to the doctor that next day. I had to advocate for myself to make sure I received a mammogram. Once again, I was told, "you're young, and there's probably nothing to worry about. But because of your family history, we will schedule a mammogram." They performed the test. I was told the results looked concerning and that I needed a biopsy. August 30th, I heard the words no one wants to hear, "Ms. McLean, it is a cancer. It's at least clinical stage 3, which is why under your arm is swollen." I sat there with my mom in shock. I had a talk with God. "Lord, I don't know how you are going to fix this. But I know you will fix this because no one is raising my daughter but me." My mother hugged me tightly and pleaded the blood of Jesus over my life. My boyfriend had come to Williamsburg to help watch my daughter while I went to that doctor's visit. When I returned home I fell face-first on the bed as I told him I had cancer. I missed my family reunion that year and remembered my cousin asking if I felt better. I remember telling her, "Well, my cold is gone…now if I can just get my head wrapped around this cancer diagnosis I just got…." I sent a text to my best friend from college. She just responded, "I'm on my way." I jokingly sent a text to one of my other friends back home, and I think I almost caused her to crash her car. I sent a text to my sorority line sister. I would have fainted had I not believed.

I was told the *good news* that my cancer wasn't the aggressive form. I received a nurse navigator and went to whom they recommended. After all, I didn't know anyone. I didn't receive my scans until the middle of September. My oncologist was the best. I still have his voicemail where he told me it has not spread to the rest of my body. I had a date to start treatment, but first, I needed a port and had to see if I could get my eggs harvested since chemo normally puts many women in menopause. It's not known if you will regain the ability to have more children. Everyone doesn't have the discounted price of $6,000 to harvest eggs. Chemo treatments put me in another head space when it comes to money. I'm grateful for good insurance. The day came when I needed to get my port placed. I had the surgery and didn't feel well after. When I got to the hospital, I learned that the failed attempt to place my port had punctured my lung. They asked if I had eaten. I told them I just had a hotdog because I felt I would be there for a while. That was when I learned they can't put you to sleep with food on your stomach. My sorority line sister called me as they were rolling me to ICU. I remember telling her how impeccable her timing was. After a while, they figured out how to not have me in as deep of a sleep, and I spent the next four days in ICU on a morphine drip. I couldn't press the drip enough to handle the pain of the chest tube that came out of my side. I woke up and thought I was having an out-of-body experience, as I saw my line sister sitting by my bed, ensuring I was okay. Once discharged from the hospital, I knew I had to find a surgeon. My new surgeon was known to be the best surgeon in town. I shared my story. I told him I would sit in the waiting room and wait. I'll never forget when he told me, "You have an interesting story. You never want to be interesting to a doctor." I can laugh about it now. It wasn't funny then. I went through 8 rounds of chemotherapy over 16 weeks. Because my lump was so large, I had to have chemo first to shrink the tumor before surgically removing it. Chemo was hard. I went to the barber with my boyfriend, and he and I got matching buzz cuts. My hair fell out shortly after. The nausea required a nausea patch. I had sores inside my mouth that required a special numbing mouthwash to be able to eat. I had a leopard tongue. The nurses had never seen that before, and I let them look at it for their case study. They said it was due to toxicity. I was told I couldn't do a lot of natural foods because they may counter the poison. I had to take a shot after chemo to get my white blood cells increased after chemo. I was fortunate to be able to work 50% of the time. My boyfriend proposed in September, and we got married that November. I offered him an out because I didn't know if I would survive the chemo, and I didn't know how I would change from this experience. He attended every chemo, and I was appreciative of his support.

I completed chemo in January 2014. I made a poster with "Eight is Enough," and my mom and daughter rang the bell with me. My husband was there as well. After my blood count numbers returned to some normalcy, I chose to have a bilateral mastectomy. I wore a large G cup bra size prior to surgery; having a lumpectomy (removing only the cancer lump) would leave me uneven. My initial plan was to cut off both breasts and have a Diep flap surgery after radiation. This is where they surgically move tissue from another part of your body and create new breasts. For some reason, I wasn't nervous. I just wanted cancer out of my body. They performed the surgery. My job gave me an awesome care basket. I was shocked that I didn't stay longer than 24 hours and had great home health. Once I recovered, I endured 33 rounds of radiation. Yes, my skin burned. At round 31, I visited my oncologist, who said… (paraphrased), "We couldn't find your original pathology results, so with your mastectomy, we ran another report. It turns out your initial diagnosis was incorrect. You do have HER2 as well." I asked, "Okay, what exactly does that mean?" Simply put, I had another cancer that had not been treated. Since I had my port removed during the mastectomy, I had to get another. I returned to treatment for another year of chemo. The only positive was that I felt better about missing my diagnosis. Due to HER2 being so aggressive, it could've been easier to miss stages one and two during self-exams. The chemo caused my oxygen levels to drop so badly that I had to use an oxygen tank. I couldn't travel to three funerals of men who were like fathers to me. After the diagnosis and new round of surgeries, I decided I didn't want anyone else cutting me ever, and I decided I would be flat and fabulous, without breasts. I have prosthetics for all occasions. It's amazing the type of available accessories.

Beyond the scars to the healing

There are residual effects that you don't understand as you are enduring this struggle. There are mental struggles as everything that makes you a woman is killing you - from the uterus that carries the baby to the breasts that feed them to the estrogen that is feeding the cancer. And the way to fix it is to take away everything that makes you a woman. I had to look into the treatments after chemo to ensure the cancer stays at bay. There are pills with side effects that can include death. I tried the first set of pills. They caused uterine changes, and I changed to a shot. The shot was okay, but it didn't stop any estrogen. I had an oophorectomy that created the side effects of instant menopause. My hormones were off balance. I am pre-diabetic. My thyroid function is out of range. I was diagnosed with asthma and anemia. My feet struggle with neuropathy. I wear a compression sleeve on my arm to prevent lymphedema. I learned that I should've been vegan and that the chemo is probably why I had to have four kidney stone surgeries. Vitamin deficiency is a concern. The new normal strains your family. I used to have the strength to do it all. Now I am good if I can wake up and work a full eight-hour day. The house isn't as clean as I want it to be. I worry about my child being okay because she watched me go through it, which traumatized her. My marriage was strained. I experienced an attitude shift. Stuff I used to care about and, once stressed over, doesn't stress me anymore. It's not that I don't care, but what I care about must be worth caring. That includes items that could break your relationship with your significant other. I would have fainted had I not believed.

Cancer is an everyday struggle. I don't have breasts. I check my breast wall regularly to make sure I don't feel any signs of the cancer returning. I wonder if the cancer has metastasized to my bones with every pain. I've watched friends die from this disease. I had friends and family tell me to "stay strong. God will take care of you. It's going to be alright." But when I was going through it, it all sounded cliché. I have faith. I stayed repeating Psalm 27:13, "*I would have fainted had I not believed I would experience the goodness of the Lord in the land of the living.*" I believe it will all be okay. I don't want anyone else raising my child but me. I understood that part. But if your body had never been affected like what I was going through, I didn't want to hear it. Not even from my mother, who is also a survivor. To me, her issues were different. She was older. She didn't have concerns about wanting more children. So here I sit with no possibility of carrying another child and a diminished dream of using my $6000 embryos.

Looking up, I realized perspective is important. I became an ambassador through my journey, and for a short time, I served as a facilitator for a Breast Health Nonprofit Organization, not only to help others but to cope. Watching people I love die became so hard and traumatizing that I had to step away for a while and learn to heal. I knew that my daughter felt what I felt. If I see it as trauma, she will be (and has been) traumatized. Being a mother, daughter, and wife, as a caregiver, I have to also take care of myself first. As airlines instruct their passengers, I must put on my own oxygen mask before I try to assist others. I learned that although I can't sing a strong alto, a strong tenor is still needed. It's important to live every moment as if it's your last because it may be. Don't wait until you are older to enjoy life. Older may not come. Don't stress over the small things that really don't matter. I learned that opportunities to help others with this testimony may save a life. Many times, you feel alone, even with a strong village. However, you are not. Sharing your testimony with others may open doors to a totally new life if you let it. As of this writing, it has been almost nine years of clean scans. Every birthday, I travel to a body of water to celebrate another opportunity to experience life.

Note to Self:

Never forget that perspective is important. You got here believing you would see the goodness of the Lord in the land of the living. So continue to share your testimony, and help others know they, too, can believe.

Biblical Reference:

Psalm 27:13 | ¹³ I had fainted, unless I had believed to see the goodness of the LORD in the land of the living.

Chapter Definitions for Medical Terms

DIEP Flap: In a DIEP flap, fat, skin, and blood vessels are cut from the wall of the lower belly and moved up to your chest to rebuild your breast.

This information is provided by Breastcancer.org. Donate to support free resources and programming for people affected by breast cancer.

Radiation: Therapy Radiation therapy (radiotherapy) is a treatment that uses high-energy radiation to kill cancer cells and shrink tumors.

This information is provided by Breastcancer.org. Donate to support free resources and programming for people affected by breast cancer.

In **HER2**-positive breast cancer, the HER2 (human epidermal growth factor receptor 2) gene doesn't work correctly and makes too many copies of itself. These extra HER2 genes make too many proteins known as HER2 receptors. These HER2 receptors are like ears, or antennae, on the surface of the breast cells. The HER2 receptors receive signals that stimulate the cell to grow and multiply. But breast cancer cells with too many HER2 receptors can pick up too many growth signals. This makes breast cells grow and divide too fast in an uncontrolled way.

This information is provided by Breastcancer.org. Donate to support free resources and programming for people affected by breast cancer.

Port: A device used to draw blood and give treatments, including intravenous fluids, blood transfusions, or drugs such as chemotherapy and antibiotics. The port is placed under the skin, usually in the right side of the chest. It is attached to a catheter (a thin, flexible tube) that is guided (threaded) into a large vein above the right side of the heart called the superior vena cava. A needle is inserted through the skin into the port to draw blood or give fluids and other treatments. A port may stay in place for many weeks, months, or years. Also called port-a-cath.
https://www.cancer.gov/

oophorectomy
(oh-oh-foh-REK-toh-mee)
Surgery to remove one or both ovaries.
https://www.cancer.gov/

neuropathy
(noor-AH-puh-thee)

A nerve problem that causes pain, numbness, tingling, swelling, or muscle weakness in different parts of the body.
https://www.cancer.gov/

<u>metastasis</u>
(meh-TAS-tuh-sis)
The spread of cancer cells from the place where they first formed to another part of the body.
https://www.cancer.gov/

UNTIL IT'S DIFFERENT

Erica "Lala" Morgan
(Cancer Survivor)

I have always been fluffy and have been since I had my children. They and my mom are my backbone and hold me up when I am at my weakest. If they were able to take my pain away, I know they would because they tell me time and time again that they would without question. I say that just to lead to this. I had unsolicited advice, often. When I was told I had this disease inside my body, I wanted it out *immediately*! When people find out you have Cancer, they like to offer *unsolicited* advice. You know, slick-ish like, *you know sugar feeds Cancer, maybe you should exercise and eat better*. Then I let loose my split second, off-the-cuff (edited for the sake of this book) response...."Keep your comments, unwanted and unsolicited advice to your damn self." I was fuming, and they knew it, and from that day to this one, they have never spoken to me again, like I actually offended them. I, who has just been diagnosed with a life-altering disease, wanted no comments from an idiot.

I imagined having a conversation with God and asking him; how I could change this outcome; and how I could change this chapter of my life to not include the word that no individual ever wants to hear. How? At that moment, I realized I had just created a mini-movie in my head, and I was actually living this nightmare.

To hear that someone has been diagnosed with any form of cancer, I get a cold shiver, not down my spine but that coldness that gives me goosebumps. My first thoughts were, *say what* when I heard my initial diagnosis. I said, "show me what you mean?" The doctor left the room for a few minutes, and they felt like they were moving in slow motion. My ears were blocked like I couldn't hear anything else until he returned. I was scared and lost. My life had changed in a split second,...*forever*. He proceeded to show me what looked like an X-ray of my left breast. He compared the first mammogram I took a few days before to the one I took two days ago. Hell, they looked the same to me. He placed them on that wall light thingy that helps to see the X-ray a little clearer. He pointed to the first little white specks in a specific area. He had the same white specks, but there were more of them. He said that I was looking at a picture of my milk ducts and the specks were a calcification that was not normal. So, I said, "just tell me what you see in layman's terms... IS IT CANCER?" He was shocked, but I didn't care. He said that I had *Atypical Ductal Hyperplasia*, a precancerous condition. He said, Miss Brown, "there are treatments available that we can do." I turned around, confused, and said, "Who the hell is Miss Brown?" I requested another doctor who could tell me what the hell was going on! This radiologist looked at me, "I'm sorry but are you saying you're not Miss Brown?" At this point, another doctor entered the room and asked if he could help. "Please do, because he doesn't know if I have cancer or if Miss Brown does!" I gave him my identifiers, and both left the room. After returning, he apologized for the mix-up, but I was livid. After verifying my identity, he told me my next steps. I needed a biopsy and to schedule an appointment with a surgeon. I wanted to know why. Cancer was possible, but if it was, it was in its early stages.. However, a *Static Needle Biopsy* was the only way to know definitively. I left that little office; in that big hospital, scared and uncertain about what lay ahead. I sat in my car for two hours crying and trying to get my mind right to function behind the wheel. Crying was the new normal until I knew the outcome of that biopsy. This felt like the darkest day of my entire life.

Upon my official diagnosis, I endured six weeks of radiation therapy. After six weeks of being burned, my skin looked like leather and I was uncomfortable and ugly. 42 days of feeling like I had been nuked by a chemical of some kind and oh, did I say, feeling and looking *ugly*! I didn't want anyone to see me. I wanted to hide from people and just fade away.

I hated what I saw in the mirror when I got in and out of the shower. I hated the lasting effects and limitations I had to endure for a lifetime. This time in my life required numerous doctor visits and blood work. My surgeon even asked if I wanted to be tested to see if I had the BRCA gene. This was something that I considered a life-or-death situation as far as I was concerned. I am the first woman in my family on both sides to be diagnosed with breast cancer, and I am a mother of three adult women to whom I could have possibly given this horrible disease to. But things got better because I was *not* a carrier, and my daughters were safe! Telling about this part of my journey makes me happy because I didn't pass that nasty gene to my girls. There was a time when I couldn't actually say the word. Every time I tried, I cried. When people asked how I was, I cried when people looked at me with those pitiful eyes. You know the look, when they don't know the exact words to say, so they look at you with sadness and that poor baby look. I am here to tell you that no survivor wants your pity. We fight with every ounce of strength and dignity we have. When I finished radiation, I had to learn how to live with the deformity of my body. Accepting the *"new"* me took a while, but to see who emerged on the other side of this thing was gorgeous and still beautifully and wonderfully made.

Cancer not only changes *your* life, but it alters established and those developing.

Proclaiming Wholeness Beyond The Blemishes Of Cancer

1. Cancer changes your body forever. I know it firsthand; because I live with it like millions of people daily.

2. It makes you rewrite your entire outlook on life. Makes you grateful for genuine relationships, family, hugs and kisses, and a gentle touch. The ability to draw in a long deep breath without the help of a machine is priceless.

3. Intimacy is different for both individuals. Your partner is scared to touch you for fear of hurting you. You are apprehensive because you feel ugly and may still be experiencing discomfort. So if you want to make it work, you must keep trying until you find your groove.

4. It affects your cash flow negatively. In most cases, you are not able to work. Therefore, bills pile up, and before you know it, you're struggling. There are programs out there that can assist, but they are minimal.

5. You ask, *why me*, more times than you can recall. This is still my question, and I still don't have an answer.

Today I see things differently. But sometimes, I revert to that wound when I hear of someone passing from any illness. Life and surviving cancer will always be different until it's not.

Note to Self:

Always remember that life is worth living no matter how hard and fast the obstacles are thrown at you. So be like Ali,

"Float like a Butterfly, and Sting like a Bee"

Chapter Definitions for Medical Terms

Atypical Ductal Hyperplasia: Atypical hyperplasia is a precancerous condition that affects cells in the breast. Atypical hyperplasia describes an accumulation of abnormal cells in the milk ducts and lobules of the breast. Atypical hyperplasia isn't isn't Cancer Cancer, but it increases the risk of breast cancer.

Static needle biopsy: A type of biopsy that can help to diagnose cancerous cells in breast tissue.

RESILIENCE

Leonetta Jules & Taneja Jules
(Caregiver/ Childhood Cancer Survivor)

Isaiah 61:1-3 reads, *"The Spirit of the Sovereign Lord is on me because the Lord has anointed me to proclaim good news to the poor. He has sent me to bind up the brokenhearted, to proclaim freedom for the captives and release from darkness for the prisoners, to proclaim the year of the Lord's favor and the day of vengeance of our God, to comfort all who mourn and provide for those who grieve in Zion— to bestow on them a crown of beauty instead of ashes, the oil of joy instead of mourning, and a garment of praise instead of a spirit of despair. They will be called oaks of righteousness, a planting of the Lord for the display of his splendor."*

This is my story of **Beauty for Ashes.**

When I was ten months old, I was diagnosed with a rare eye cancer called Retinoblastoma. It originates in the retina, a thin layer of nerve tissue covering the back of the eye, and allows the ability to see; due to the aggressive nature of cancer, treatment needed to begin right away to save my life and preserve my vision. I was rushed to Philadelphia within a matter of days, where I received the formal diagnosis and treatment. My options were chemotherapy, radiation therapy, and enucleation, which is removing the eye.

My parents opted for the latter due to my age because chemo and radiation were too much to put on an infant. And so, my story begins. Cancer destroyed and stole my right eye.

I learned to adapt to the world around me at an early age. My mom always said I was resilient, stubborn, strong-willed, and self-sufficient. They nicknamed me TAZ, after the Tasmanian devil, because nothing was safe when I got wound up. I was a huge ball of energy, fearless, and I didn't take any mess from anybody. In fact, my mom and dad told me about being in kindergarten and getting sent to the principal's office for trying to fight a fifth grader for talking about my eye, lol. I don't remember that, but it sounds about right to me. I was a spicy little one.

Thank God for my resilience because at the age of three, during a checkup, a heart murmur was discovered. I know that sounds weird, but they had to check my vitals because I had to be put to sleep for checkups I had every 6 months. They wanted to make sure no cancer was growing in the other eye. When I got home to Virginia after that visit, I was followed for two years by a cardiologist for a congenital heart defect that was found. I was diagnosed with pulmonary stenosis (a narrowing of the valve located between the lower right heart chamber (right ventricle) and the lung arteries (pulmonary arteries). This caused me to have chronic pneumonia at least twice a year, sometimes more, because it kept blood from flowing properly to my lungs. I also had an atrial septal defect (a hole in the heart between the heart's upper chambers (atria)). The defect was believed to be linked to a gene mutation which may have caused the Retinoblastoma. The heart defect eventually developed into congestive heart failure. I had open heart surgery to close the hole and correct the displaced valves that were keeping proper blood flow from getting to my lungs. During the procedure, they found a vein typically gone after birth but never did. The vein had scar tissue that caused a blockage, and within a few months, I was in the hospital after complaining of headaches. I was suffering from an aneurysm that was on the verge of rupturing. I was only five years old.

At the start of first grade, I had a prosthetic right eye and a pretty fresh scar from open-heart surgery. It wasn't pretty and was visible when I wore certain shirts. It made me the target of bullying throughout my entire school career and home life with friends outside. It bothered me, but I was tough and never let it get to me. My momma always told me, "Never let them see you sweat; never let them know they're getting to you because they will never let up," so I didn't. I could come back word for word and run with the best of them. I was more than capable of living up to my nickname TAZ!

When I got to middle school, however, the bullying intensified. It went from a couple of kids teasing me here and there to what seemed to be the whole world against me. That coupled with having a learning disability, at times, it felt that I didn't have a friend in the world. I would tell the teachers, and it only got worse. My mom tried to involve the principals, counselors, and civic and social groups, but nothing worked. I really felt like I didn't want to go on living. Finally, the verbal bullying became physical, and the teachers sometimes blamed me for bringing it on myself. Can you believe that? I was an awkward kid trying to find my place where there wasn't one. I couldn't see then that sometimes being different and not fitting is a setup for greatness. But I'm getting ahead of myself. So now, not only had cancer stolen my eye and left me a scar from open heart surgery, it had destroyed my self-esteem and self-worth due to the severe bullying I had become a victim too.

I often found a way of escape through drawing and designing clothes. I loved to dress up and find different ways to revamp clothes. From a kid at about 2 years old, I would twist and turn things into an outfit and parade it in front of my parents and sisters. Nothing was safe, clothes, towels, bed sheets, curtains, bed canopies; it didn't matter, I was making an outfit or dress out of it. My mom told me about when I was in first grade, and I would sleep so hard in the mornings that she could wash me up and get me dressed, all while I was still asleep. I would get on the bus and fall back to sleep, so I would not even know what I was wearing most of the time until I got to class and took off my coat, lol. My teachers knew how much I loved clothes and fashion and dressing up, so they found a way to make sure I woke up to do my morning work. She told me that I could do a mini fashion show for my classmates if I finished my work. So that's how they got me to do my work every day, and my mom always made sure she dressed me up extra cute. My mom had a way of jazzing up those uniform outfits like nobody's business. One day my mom reached out to two beautiful ladies in charge of doing fashion week in our state. She showed them my designs and told them what I struggled with regarding my self-esteem. We met and clicked instantly, and they allowed me to be a designer in their show. I went on to travel to New York, Baltimore, New Jersey, and more. I met celebrities, and I really had a ball. It was a real self-esteem booster. The kids at school didn't really start treating me any better because of all the places I traveled and where I started going and started doing. What did happen, though, was that *I found out who I was!* My world didn't just exist within the walls of my school, and my worth wasn't predicated on what others thought of me. I realized that my worth lay directly in God's eyes and the mind when I became who He created me to be. I no longer design clothes and travel the country doing fashion shows; it served the purpose it was supposed to at a time when I needed it. I have now found a new passion in cooking, but I am passionate about helping other kids discover who they are. I enjoy helping other kids learn to stand up against bullies and never let anyone dim their light. I am passionate about being a friend to those who are friendless. I find so much beauty in allowing others to have the space to be their genuine selves with no condemnation but the freedom to love themselves unconditionally. That's the best weapon against any bully!

Moment of Inspiration

Jeremiah 29:11 reads, "For I know the plans I have for you," declares the Lord, "plans to prosper you and not to harm you, plans to give you hope and a future." This means knowing that God has a plan for your life. Nothing that takes place has caught him by surprise. Everything you go through and come out of is part of a grand design meant to lead you toward your greatness. It's okay to be tired, it's okay to feel hopeless sometimes, and it's okay to grow weary in the struggles and in the fight. These are all real human emotions that are part of the process. To heal properly, you must feel and work through all of them. The important thing to remember is to never stay where you are. Don't ever get comfortable with feeling in your low state. Talk to someone, seek therapy, pray, consult your support system, and endure until your change comes. The tough times don't always last. Light and better days are coming, and God has a plan for your life that will give you hope and a future. Delight yourself in him, and he will guide you toward your greater.

Note to Self:

Dear little me, I know you are having the time of your life right now. I want you to know that tough times are coming. People are not going to understand you; they will mistreat you, and they will say some unkind things to you too. Some days will come when you have pain because of some things you will experience in your body and mind. What I want you to always remember is to *keep going*! Push forward, do your work in school, know your worth (you are priceless), ignore the haters; they won't even matter in the future, pay attention to the lessons you learn from them, and always stick up for yourself. You are great beyond measure; you are awesome beyond your wildest dreams. Your quirks, personality, awkward ways, and kind heart will take you places you never even dreamed of going. The very things that are coming to break you down and destroy you will cause you to rise above everything and be great! When it is all said and done, you will be able to gain *beauty* for your *ashes!*

Chapter Definition for Medical Terms

Retinoblastoma: a rare eye cancer that is found during childhood. It originates in the retina, which is a thin layer of nerve tissue that covers the back of the eye and gives the eye the ability to see.

Chemotherapy: Treatment that uses drugs to stop the growth of cancer cells, either by killing the cells or stopping them from dividing.

Radiation Therapy: This cancer treatment uses high doses of radiation to kill cancer cells and shrink tumors.

Enucleation is the removal of the eye from orbit. It involves separating all tissue connections between the globe and the orbit.

Atrial Septal Defect: a hole in the heart between the upper chambers (atria)

Pulmonary Stenosis: A condition in which the pulmonary valve is too tight, so that blood flow from the heart's right ventricle into the pulmonary artery is impeded.

Pneumonia: lung inflammation caused by a bacterial or viral infection in which the air sacs fill with pus and may become solid.

Aneurysm: when part of an artery wall weakens, allowing it to abnormally balloon out or widen. If not treated, rupturing is possible, which can cause internal bleeding and possible death.

SHE CALLED ME ANGEL FACE

Amber Curtis
(Daughter of a Butterfly)

My mom's name is Dawn Hughes; when she died, she was 46. My older sister was 22, I was 14, and my younger sister was 11. Growing up, she was my only parent— the only parent any of us had. She worked five jobs and still had all the time in the world for us. I never really understood how she could do everything she needed to do and still have time for us until I got older. Then, when I was 12, she was diagnosed with Colon Cancer; she fought for her life and our lives for the next two and a half years- she went into remission. Still, she ended up passing away on September 6th, 2014. I have left out so many gruesome stories and cruel details because even though her battle was brutal, and she's no longer with us, she absolutely won.

My Mom taught me to be a role model. Sometimes a good role model is all someone has. When she got sick, she got me to go to a summer camp with other kids who had parents diagnosed with cancer. It greatly impacted my life; I gained new friends who understood, I gained a new perspective on life, that made dealing with it all easier; I also gained a new support system that I didn't have before. After I turned 18, I became a counselor. It was so refreshing and reassuring to know that I made a difference every day I spent with kids just like me. Whether it was just listening or giving advice, laughing, crying, or singing with them— it showed them that they weren't alone and that it's okay to not always have good days.

The hardest lesson from my mom that I had to learn was to love myself but to also appreciate and indulge in the true me- because if I don't, how can I expect others to? My Dad wasn't around until I was 12 and was gone again before I was 15. So my mom never had a person to do life with besides us. But she seemed okay with that. We were the reason she had a great life. We were all she needed. Regardless of who I was- whether I was a nerd or a jock- my mom always reminded me of how important I was. She reminded me that I was beautiful, strong-willed, bold, empathetic, and genuine, and that all of these traits were to be appreciated, not taken for granted. My sisters and I argued a decent amount growing up as most siblings do- and my mom was always so adamant about being nicer to each other. Whenever we bickered about something dumb, she'd say, "girls, there's enough evil in the world... cut it out." When I was younger, I never really thought too much of it because they're my sisters, and they made me angry 98% of the time. But, since I've gotten older, I realized how extensively true that was. With mom getting sick and later passing, my sisters were the only people I had. We experienced the sides of that fight, so it was insanely counterproductive to be against each other. Not only did we have to watch the strongest woman we knew fight for her life, but we also had to deal with growing up with life's evils. Bullying, abuse, pride, manipulation, and puberty; were things that made a hard life even more difficult.

"Mom. You have no idea what you're talking about. You're wrong. That's not true. That's not what's going on," we said to her. But every piece of advice she gave me rang true on more than one occasion. And even now- eight years later- I take a little more time to appreciate the things she shared. I never really understood how much I took for granted. I am so very grateful for everything she gave me. Sometimes I really wish I could just look her in the face and tell her she was right- about everything. There are so many times that something happens like she said it would, and I want to just call her and tell her all about it. So often, I want to just call her, hear her voice, get her advice, and actually listen to what she has to say. She knew what she was talking about; I should've listened more often.

If I could have one more conversation with my mom, I would tell her that I appreciate her and her guidance, as well as her suffering and sacrifices for all three of us. That I missed her physically being at homecoming, prom, and graduation. I'll miss her physical presence at my wedding, the birth of my future children, and every other day too. I'd tell her that I knew she was there with me in every way she could be. I would thank her for my individuality and for showing me how to appreciate that about myself. I would tell her how much I think about her and how much she means to me. I'd tell her that I love her a million times and that although she isn't here anymore, she will always be a part of me.

Note to Self:

If I could tell my younger self anything, it would be to love the quirks/oddities/differences I have because they are rare traits and something to be appreciated. I say even though they always say it never *gets easier*. Some days just get better, and you learn to turn the bad into good. It's okay to cry— it doesn't make you weak; it's okay to have bad days. It makes you human; it's okay to put yourself first because you can't take care of everyone else if you don't take care of yourself. I would tell the younger me that even if you feel alone, you're not— and you're damn sure not a burden. Do NOT apologize for being too much, too bossy, or too mature for your age. You made it through hell and back, and you're still standing. One day you won't cry as hard or as often; you will find people who love you unconditionally, and when you do- accept it because you deserve it.

THE SUNDAY BEFORE
11.24.19.21.36

Michelle Wicker & Jordynne Wicker
(Caregiver/Granddaughter of a Butterfly)

The Sunday Before

Michelle Wicker

Somehow, in some way, if my family is to change, it seems to happen on a Sunday.

My daughter and I were living in Japan when our lives changed. We had been there for less than a year when one of the largest recorded earthquakes in the world shook our world. There were so many unknowns at the time. Do we leave or stay? Can I send her back to the states, and who would I send her with if I did? I listened to science, and I talked with my parents. Finally, we took all of the necessary precautions and stayed.

The following month our world shook again – but this time, our foundations were shaken to their very cores.

We received the news that my father had stage four lung cancer. Again, there were so many unknowns and questions. But the only thing we could do – from the other side of the world – was to again listen to the science, the doctors and talk with my parents. My father – who I have always called Daddy – was always a supporter of us spreading our wings. He told us to stay in Japan – so we did, for the next seven years.

In 2017 it was time for us to move. I asked my job to move me back home to Virginia or at least to the east coast. I knew my daddy's health was not improving, and I wanted to be closer to my parents. So they moved us to Washington state.

Two years later, in the spring/summer, I received a call from my mother. She had been diagnosed with breast cancer. She was going to begin chemo and radiation. And my father was to begin hospice care. Our foundation and our world were shaken again. However, before we could get home, I had to put some things in place. First, my daughter had to finish 8th grade. Then I had to make arrangements with work to take an extended leave of absence. I trained an assistant manager to handle things while I was gone. I also needed to find someone to stay at our house and take care of our dog and fish. I then paid my utilities and rent ahead of time to cover the months of our absence. Lastly, I got a power of attorney for the person staying in my house and driving my car. Thank God for good friends! Once everything was arranged and in place, and school was over, we packed our clothes and left for Virginia. We got home at the end of June 2019.

We were there to help my mother. In all she was going through, she never skipped a beat. We quickly found a routine that worked for each of us. We went through the days in shifts. My mother tended to be up early, and I was up late. My daddy was up at what seemed like at all times. His bed was set up in the den – right next to the kitchen and where my mother spent most of her time. We ate, cooked, talked, socialized, and watched tv with him. We enjoyed his company, and (I hope) he enjoyed ours. As those months progressed – he would need help with daily activities such as eating, drinking, and using the bathroom. Thank goodness he had a hospice nurse – who assisted with shaving and bathing. I was very thankful for my daughter – who helped with any and every task she was presented with. At the tender age of fourteen, she did and saw things that no child should have to see or do.

In those last five months, memories were created that will last us a lifetime. Images were forged in my mind that I easily recall. Growing up, I was always a Daddy's girl – so those months were hard for me and yet joyous at the same time. I saw the man I witnessed to be so strong – become someone different. I saw the man with strong opinions and a lot to say – struggling to ask for a cup of water. I saw the man that used to carry me on his shoulders build structures and fly airplanes – needed help holding a fork. I saw a man that could cut yards and walk on rooftops – required help getting up from bed and standing. I saw a man like no other – succumb to the ills of this world. His transition became the hardest to endure and a guessing game. Sometimes we could not help him simply because we did not know what he wanted. We know that it was a challenge for him to express himself. As a result, tears of anger were shed because we could not communicate. Then, those tears transitioned to ones of sadness because I simply could not help him.

On a Sunday night, I heard my mother cry out as my daddy took his final breaths. I will never forget that sound or the day my daddy completed his journey. As the family gathered around him, I went to wake up my brother, who was deaf and was asleep. As I went to wake him and we returned to the family, my father took his final breath. I will never forget the Sunday before Thanksgiving (like Sundays before when his younger brother passed, and his own father passed [my uncle and Grandfather]).

Words of Encouragement: I felt helpless being on the other side of the world and receiving news like we did. At the same time, I know that if we had returned to my parents when daddy was first diagnosed – we would have truly been helpless. I could have done nothing more by his side than I did when I was in Japan. I always knew that God would put me where he needed me when he needed me to be there. And God did just that.

Always have faith. Never let that go. God knows what he is doing even though we may not see it or feel it at the time. So hold on tight to the fact that God is there for you. Know, too, that God will provide. Being a child and a parent simultaneously – I had many responsibilities. Sometimes I didn't know what I would do or how to make it all work. But God did. He had it all planned out. I just needed to listen and experience the journey. That was all I could do. So hold on to that faith, and hold on to your loved ones.

Looking back, perhaps my daddy did not want us there at the beginning. Maybe he did not want us to see what he was going to go through. Perhaps he wanted the images we had of him to be what would stay with us forever, and they will. I also know that I will see him again. I have faith in that. Hold on to your faith tighter than you've ever held on to anything else.

Note to Self:

Keep that faith. And HUG. All I could think about was feeling his arms around me during the time I spent with my father. Knowing that I would never get to hug him again once he passed. HUG. Hug your loved ones. Hug tight. Hug for a long time. Don't be the first to let go. HUG. Keep hugging…

11.24.19.21.36

Jordynne Wicker

I am the grandchild of a butterfly that is currently flying high. But that butterfly was more than just a grandfather to me. That butterfly was a father figure and someone I called Daddy.

In 2011 my butterfly was diagnosed with lung cancer. At the time, I was only six years old and didn't know much. I didn't even know what cancer was or how big of a deal it could be. All I knew was that he was sick. As time passed, things only got worse, as they sometimes do with a cancer diagnosis. I quickly learned he wasn't going to get any better. So in the summer of 2019, when I was 14, I traveled from Washington state to Norfolk, Virginia, to help my grandmother take care of my daddy. He had decided to stop treatment and enter hospice. My grandmother had also been diagnosed with breast cancer and was set to begin radiation treatment. Within five months of living in Virginia and helping my grandmother and Daddy, I started high school, joined several sports teams, and began to notice boys.

We knew it was only a matter of days during his last week. Since we knew he did not have much longer, we wanted to call family and let them know. We called my mom to return home from Washington state (she had flown back for a brief period for work). We called my uncle who lived hours away. Then we called my grandmother's sister to come down from Northern Virginia. On November 24 at 9:36 pm, I watched him take his last breath as my grandmother held his hand crying.

He was not pronounced dead till an hour later when the nurse arrived. But the time 9:36pm will always be burned into my brain as that is the time I saw when I looked up at the clock as he left the place and went to a much better one where he was no longer sick or in pain.

I have always been fascinated with tattoos and wanted some of my own. However, before I do anything big in my life, I like to research the pros and cons. In November of 2021, two years later, I got the tattoo 11.24.19.21.36 on my back right shoulder. It is a date (November 24, 2019) and time (9:36pm) that will always hold significance in my heart as it is when my butterfly left this world.

Occasionally, people will ask about the significance of the numbers, and I tell them. It always makes me laugh when their facial expression changes because it's not what they expected. People try to even

There Is Beauty Beyond The Scars

guess, coming up with coordinates or just a random sequence of numbers. But when people ask, it's my reminder that he is closer to me, even when I forget.

The following month after his passing, my grandmother went into remission after battling her own journey with breast cancer. As a result, we held his memorial service in January 2020, 5 days after my birthday.

My tattoo is significant because it is the first death I have experienced in person. Over the years, there have been several deaths in my family. Living overseas and being so young have prevented me from being there in person and being able to properly grieve the loss of loved ones.

Holding his hand and watching him take his last breath was a lot to experience, At any age. Death takes a toll on people in many ways, and sometimes those first few seconds after can matter the most. That was, in fact, the case for me. Those first few seconds after my butterfly left this earth, I didn't know how to feel. One thing I remember the most was that I didn't cry like everyone else. I was just kind of there. I tried my best to comfort those around me and help the nurse collect the unused meds when she finally arrived. Still, I didn't cry till later when I finally got ready to sleep. Those few seconds after me just being there and trying to help, I also just watched. We couldn't do anything till the nurse arrived, so I watched the clock while waiting. That is how I knew when he took his final breath and an hour later when the nurse finally came. My tattoo reminds me that just because I didn't know what to feel in the moment doesn't mean I can't have or feel those feelings later. Grief has no end date or timeline; it comes and goes at its own pace and wherever you are.

By this time, it's been almost three years since his death, and I'm still not done grieving. My hormones and emotions are all over the place at seventeen, so my grief most definitely comes and goes in waves.

Words of Encouragement from Jordynne:

Grief is different for everyone at any age and at any time of life. Just because you don't cry, or maybe you're not angry by day five, doesn't mean you're not grieving or that you're not doing it right. Maybe someone moves on from a loss before you, and that's ok! Grief takes time and is on no timeline.

A loss is a loss regardless of whether it is a loved one, a security blanket, or a home. Different types of loss will certainly affect everyone in different ways. Different types of loss will allow everyone to experience their own forms of grief in their own time and own ways.

It takes time, patience, understanding, and lots of support. If you feel you do not have those things on your own or at home, there are grieving support groups that can provide help. It allows them to share their stories and let you know you are not alone.

Grief isn't forever, but it also isn't a 5-step process for everyone to go through.

SHE PERSISTED

Melody Hansley
(Daughter of a Butterfly)

Persistence is a good quality to have. It requires the ability to carry on in the midst of difficulty. I cannot count the number of times that my dear mother chose to persist instead of selecting to give up. My mother was a primary example of someone driven to live life in spite of having been diagnosed with Colon Cancer. When I was a young girl, my mother would hold her stomach in pain and still push through to do normal activities to care for her family. I can vividly remember my mother with her long jet-black hair, smooth, soft glowing skin, and beautiful smile. I can recall the gracefulness she exuded after being given her scary diagnosis. It must have been difficult that day at her doctor's appointment hearing the words, *"You have cancer?"* Only those who have had that unfortunate or similar experience can truly understand the fear of hearing those three words. No one wants to hear them, not for themselves or anyone they love and care for. If you are reading this and you have heard those awful words, or if you've ever had anyone close and dear to you, who has listened to

There Is Beauty Beyond The Scars

those three words, then you can surely relate to the ability to persist beyond because you are here.

Most children desire a warm, loving, and caring mother. I was blessed to have one. My mother loved God and could seemingly love the hurt right out of a person. She did it numerous times for me. In addition, mother was a soft-spoken woman who loved leaving inspirational messages for others. She would always try to brighten up the day for those around her, whether it was colleagues, church members, friends or family. It wasn't until I'd turned twenty-five years old that Cancer returned to my mother's precious body, spreading from organ to organ, that I would observe my mother's strength at an all-time high. She worked for as long as possible until her body would no longer allow her to. She was denied help from Social Security Disability and had to beg a local medical company for a wheelchair for mobility. As I watched my mother lay on her dying bed, stricken with Metastatic Cancer, fighting the unbearable pains that passed through her body, she would continuously show love and care for others. My mother was a witness to people right from her bedside. She would speak life to those who would call or come to visit her. Multiple times, I witnessed my mother say to so many people, "I won't complain." Now, she may not have complained, but I can't say that I didn't complain-because I did. I felt what was happening to my dear mother was unfair.

You may have felt those feelings about your diagnosis and the diagnosis and sickness of those you love and care for. You may also be thinking, *"How can someone who is dying in pain from cancer be a witness to others?"*

I'll tell you how; As a person who lived a good life, a life of love and devotion to God and to family, as a person who had a faith strong enough to believe God for a miracle time and time again, as a person who was determined to not give up on her life until she had seen her prayers for her children answered. She persisted-she continued firmly in spite of a difficult opposition. No one is ever prepared for what Cancer brings to their lives and to the lives of their loved ones. Life will seem to be falling apart as if it has been turned completely upside down. Coping with the changes can be overwhelming, causing hopelessness and helplessness. The feelings you feel when trying to adjust to the new normal in your life can feel like you are riding on an emotional roller coaster. You may laugh and then get sad all at the exact moment. You may feel anger and regret. You may not even know what you are feeling some days. All of these feelings are normal. It is during those dark moments, those lonely moments. and those times when you feel like no one else can relate or understand the adversity you are facing, like no one else will understand the pressure and pain you are dealing with. During those moments, you must decide what you will do. Your only choices are to sit and have a pity party, and feeling sorry for yourself, your loved one, or your condition. You will have to recognize and value the opportunity you have before you, just as I had to do with my dear mother.

I'd always been told that you can't go forward looking backward, which is true. The only way to continue on with life is to look ahead. Looking ahead requires having hope. The ability to hope is the ability to believe in something better, to desire a sure thing to happen, In the case of someone experiencing Cancer that hope would be to live. So often, we tend to look at the bad. There were many times that I focused on the fact that Cancer is present, and that my loved one will have to suffer and possibly pass away soon. Instead of looking at the brighter side of things, I chose to give more attention to the negatives. Rather than focusing on the fact that although Cancer may be present, our dear loved ones are still alive and we can spend and share time with them. There was one lifesaving takeaway that I received from the journey of having to witness my mother suffer and pass away from Cancer. It was the ability to learn to transform grief into gratitude. I never knew the power of gratitude until then. It wasn't until I recognized its potential that I began to navigate life operating with gratitude instead of complaining about what my family had to lose. On the days after, whenever I couldn't see past my tears, and on the nights when I longed for a talk and gentle touch from her, in those moments when I desired motherly wisdom and advice, I had to pick myself up and set my attention on the good memories and the many things I had to be grateful for. I had to learn to appreciate both the good and the bad times, and you will have to do the same to keep from allowing the pain of loss to overtake you.

It is not easy journeying alongside someone who has to fight to live. It is tough to experience the day-to-day challenges of medical visits, and the aftermath of radiation treatments. I remember having my mother sit in my salon chair as I lay the clippers to her head and cut off what was left of her long, beautiful hair. I remember taking her shopping for a wig that she really didn't feel comfortable wearing. Doing just the most straightforward task became hard for my mother until she could no longer get out of bed. Seeing her weight drop suddenly and watching her as she became weak and fragile was probably harder than anything. I recall having to feed her just as I would a baby.

The wide-reaching effects of someone close to you having Cancer can do a lot to the caregiver mentally and emotionally. It is a good idea to surround yourself with individuals who can offer help and support you as you carry out your new tasks. The things in life that had once come so easily, became demanding challenges. And it doesn't seem to get any easier after that special someone is gone. In fact, it is more challenging to learn to live life without your person.

Here are some tips to help you move forward:

- Acknowledge, Accept by honoring the fact that your person has a Cancer diagnosis or has passed on.
- Be patient with yourself and others, allowing yourself time to grieve the new reality that has been given you.
- Find a support system where you can simply be yourself and open to the fact that you are not okay.
- Recognize that grief is a natural response to loss and it is the love you have for someone.
- Keep a journal of your feelings to help navigate through the difficult days.
- Practice having quiet time, meditate and practice the pause to simply BREATHE.
- Practice Self-Care and self-compassion.
- Talk to someone trusted, whether licensed or a friend, just talk and let it out.

I would never have imagined that I would only have my mother for a short time. I would never have thought I'd have to share photographs and tell stories to my children about their grandmother instead of having the ability to drive them over to her house for visits. Like many others, I thought I had plenty of time to enjoy her. But unfortunately, we never know when a life-changing circumstance will occur in our lives.

We must learn to live, laugh, love, and enjoy each moment offered to us. We live on borrowed time. I still hold dear and cherish a greeting card that my mother gave me, which reads, *"God grant me the SERENITY to accept the things I cannot change, the COURAGE to change the things I can, and the WISDOM to know the difference."*

I had to learn to accept the things that I could not change. Not only do those words resonate with me and help keep me going during my daily struggle of missing my mother, but they allow me to understand the prayer that she must have prayed during her battle with Cancer. Maybe she was asking God to give her the strength to accept what she could not change, and the courage to change those things she could and use her wisdom to simply be able to be okay with all that she was going through. By holding on to that valued card, I'm allowed the wonderful opportunity to look at my mother's precious handwriting inside, which helps to brighten my day.

Maybe, you have something of sentimental value that you have held onto from your loved one that keeps you filled with their love and presence. Or perhaps you are thinking of something you can create or purchase to leave behind once your earthly adventure is complete. I would encourage anyone to make all the memories they possibly can, to take as many photos, and to record as many videos as possible because life doesn't give many second chances. Because we never know how a cancer diagnosis can go, it's better to hope for the best and prepare for the opposite. Now, that may seem like you're giving into a death sentence by preparing for the worst, but that isn't the case. By making preparations, you keep from leaving your family with a ton of responsibilities.

My hope for you is that you have received some nuggets to assist you as you carry forth on your journey and that you will be able to graciously leave behind your legacy and live out your loved one's legacy, that you will be able to celebrate in the now and appreciate all that you have and the time that you have been given. I hope you keep your head up even when the days are dark and the heaviness is upon your shoulder. I hope you believe that you haven't been given this journey just to walk it alone, but to help someone else. You are more than your bout with Cancer. You are more than the scars. You are more than the heartache and pain from your sufferings. You are a miracle that is still here after all you have been through. You are a light to others, and you must forever remember that YOU ARE MORE than this battle.

May you be encouraged and let gratitude be your attitude. My hope is that you will continue to persist even through the storm. There is a rainbow waiting on the other side. Persist, press, and push through. You've got this! This, too, shall pass. The storm won't always last. The pain may not ever ultimately end, but it will lighten. Had my mother given up the fight when she was first diagnosed, I would have lost her when I was six. But because she was willing to fight and not give up, I was granted twenty more years with her because she kept the faith and hoped for a better end. I can't imagine what life would have been like for me without my mother, and my heart goes out to those who are motherless. We must cherish the time that we have. We must value every given moment. We must encourage one another and show love. My mother fought to live when she could have died. She pressed, and she prayed. She pushed through dark times, hard times, and loneliness. She didn't give up. She stayed in the fight until the end. She persisted.

Note to Self:

"It is always darkest before dawn. The only way to see the sunrise is to push through the dark nights. Keep pushing, and you will eventually see the light again. Fight to win."

I WAS GIVEN THESE MOUNTAINS

Jackinah Denise

(Cancer Survivor/Caregiver/Daughter of a Butterfly)

"I will turn all my mountains into roads, and my highways will be raised up." – Isaiah 49:11(N.I.V.)

I was given these mountains to climb to show others they can be climbed!

Dr. Maya Angelou says it best, "I do my best because I'm counting on you counting on me." When you have been given a mountain so big, you have no other choice, but to push through not just for yourself, but for everyone watching you and those not watching…for your children and your children's children…for those who will be diagnosed with a chronic illness in the future and for the butterflies (those diagnosed, but who are no longer physically here), who have deposited so many pearls of wisdom and trusted you to carry the torch.

Everyone can attest, these past few years have been difficult in many ways, and we all have learned some life-changing lessons from the pandemic. But, just as the coronavirus has affected our communities, so has cancer. Men, women, and children are being diagnosed. Daily "we," are suffering from the lasting side effects of cancer, and even though technology has made some significant improvements, we are still dying rapidly. I say, "we," because I have heard those three devastating words, "You have cancer," more than once.

This is my story of how God took me on a journey from my childhood through adulthood, one that I never planned for myself, but used everything (bad and good) that happened to give me exactly what I prayed for, love, understanding, and family.

THE BEGINNING: Growing up, cancer was all around me. My grandfather passed away from lung cancer, and my grandmother had breast cancer. One day, a favorite aunt came to Grammy's from a 12-hour shift tired, holding her upper left side, and her face looked full of pain. She walked to the back room, and after a while, I heard a loud scream, so I ran down the hall to check on her. I saw something that looked like a black hole near her left breast. She was holding it with something that looked like cotton (later found out it was gauze with peroxide on it). She had tears flowing and was white as a ghost. I was eleven when she passed, and was told she had breast cancer. A nurse by profession, my aunt spent so much time helping others to heal, but why she avoided taking care of herself to this day still puzzles me. And there's my mom. My beautiful mother heard "you have cancer" more than once. As her long luscious curls began to fall out she cried, I do believe depression was beginning to overcome her. I went with her to her appointments and listened to her doctors. Early on, I was her at-home caregiver, as she was so sick, she couldn't move without assistance. As the oldest of three children, I became a surrogate mother to my siblings. I grew up resenting her for not just getting sick, but for many of her choices I didn't understand. My bonus dad (the father who raised me) died of lung cancer, and in 2012 my biological father lost a lung also due to lung cancer. Several of my uncles have been diagnosed with bladder (now a butterfly), kidney (now a butterfly), liver/colon (now a butterfly), and prostate cancer (currently in treatment), along with several cousins that didn't make it to see their 38th birthday.

Resentment eats away at the core of any relationship. Anger, stress and bitterness are all overwhelming emotions that can cause physical damage to your body, such as chronic pain, mental health issues, high blood pressure, headaches, and even heart disease. If you don't address the resentment, it doesn't go away by itself. Instead, it metastasizes and eventually makes it impossible for healthy relationships to survive.

Proclaiming Wholeness Beyond The Blemishes Of Cancer

Because of cancer, I lost the best years of my childhood. I hated the word. I hated the disease that made many of my loved ones look weak. What is it about this horrible disease and the people I love? What is it about this six-letter word (cancer) that makes me feel no matter how far I run, it keeps catching up to me? Growing up, I felt no one, and I mean no one, was safe because cancer has shown its ugly face too many times in my life. It's like a thief in the night coming to kill, steal, and destroy not just our physical body, but our mind, heart, and soul.

Because cancer has attacked so many members of my family, I started getting mammograms at 19. A mammogram is a procedure where each of your breasts are pressed between two plastic plates, and an x-ray is taken for diagnosis and screening for breast cancer. When you get your mammogram results, you may also be told if your breasts have low or high density. Per the C.D.C., breast density reflects the amount of fibrous and glandular tissue in a woman's breasts compared with the amount of fatty tissue in the breast, as seen on a mammogram. Women with dense breasts have a higher risk of being diagnosed with breast cancer. Men can get breast cancer, too, if there's breast tissue, there is a risk.

Breast cancer is the most common cancer diagnosed among U.S. women. It is the second leading cause of death among women after lung cancer. So, if I'm being honest, I've always feared cancer would catch up to me, but like so many times in my life, I hid my fears, swept them underneath a hug rug that has been piling up since I was a little girl. I felt if I didn't think about it, then maybe, just maybe, it would not become a part of my reality. But, oh, how wrong I was.

THE NIGHTMARE BEGINS: 2014, I lost it all. My family. My health. My career. My life (so I thought). I have been having so many health issues. Thankfully with the support of my then Commanding Officer and Chain of Command, my family and I relocated back to the states after living in Japan for a couple of years. Shortly after arriving, I went to the E.R. complaining of breast pain. My breasts were so swollen I looked like Dolly Parton, but the main difference was I couldn't move, clap and dance like her, due to the severe swelling. It was extremely difficult to put my arms down or move them. I remember being told, "Ma'am, we are definitely going to admit you, but not sure where (meaning which floor) as of yet." Fast forward four days, LT (a Navy Officer who works at the Naval Hospital) comes into the room and says, "Good news Ma'am, you are being discharged." Tears immediately started flowing. I probably felt every emotion one could have felt during that very moment. He asked why I was crying, and all I could say was, "while you all wheeled me around this hospital for four days checking my heart and now discharging me because my heart is fine, NO ONE addressed the issue I complained about in the E.R., my breast!" He actually twisted his lips to say, "Ma'am, that is not a life-threatening situation; if it's a breast issue, you can make an appointment with your primary care to get a referral to mammography." I remember counting (silently) to ten a couple of times, so I didn't flip out or say anything disrespectful. But, did he, a medical professional, just say if it's a breast situation, it's not life-threatening? Did this dude even read my chart? Why did they have me fill out paperwork asking about my family history if no one was going to read it, and consider my or my family's medical history? He would have seen that I was a high risk of a patient if they did. Now, I'm just over it! I've been fighting in two different countries for doctors to listen to me to see that something just isn't right within my body, and for someone in the medical field to do the necessary test to determine exactly what was wrong with me. I felt lost, and just wanted to give up. I had to endure two more months of severe pain, yearning for help, and having to be my own advocate until I crossed paths with the right doctor to listen to my concerns. When he completed my examination, he found alarming things. He said, "Let me stop right now and type exactly what I think is going on in your chart." He sat at the computer in the examination room and did just that. So, it was he (my medical hero) who listened to my concerns, it was he who put in the referral for me to have a mammogram (that later took two months to schedule), and it was he that requested

There Is Beauty Beyond The Scars

the results that ultimately led to my greatest fear becoming a reality.

7:30AM: Even though I had survived being hit by an eighteen-wheeler truck, numerous surgeries, internal bleeding, being diagnosed with endometriosis and fibromyalgia, ectopic pregnancy where my fallopian tube was cut, leaving me no other option, but to have a hysterectomy (keeping my ovaries, not to put a 31-year-old in early menopause), and a strong family history with cancer, NOTHING and I mean NOTHING could prepare me for what was to come.

October 27, 2014, I remember this day so vividly. Getting my baby boy geared up and ready for school. He had a big test, so I ensured he had breakfast and a stress-free morning. But then the phone rang, just 15 minutes before he was to leave to catch his bus for school. I answered cheerfully, as the caller identified himself to say, "Ma'am, I know how anxious you are to get the result from your recent biopsy; well, the results are in, and you have cancer." All I can remember was dropping the phone. I don't know how many minutes passed, but I remember a knock on my bedroom door. My baby boy was giving me a heads-up that he was leaving for school. If I'm not anything else, I am a mom first and I couldn't let my bad news change the stress-free environment I had created that morning for my son. So, to hide the devastating bomb of life, I put on a mask. This mask wasn't the K95 mask we would eventually wear to protect us during the 2019-2020 coronavirus pandemic, nor the kind of mask people wear for hunting or performances. I had to put on a mask, similar to what my ancestors, the Traditional Iroquois, wore during healing rituals to hide my physical and emotional pain. I had to be his MOM. I opened my bedroom door with a smile, grabbed his hands and we prayed as we usually do every morning. I kissed and hugged him tightly, only for him to say, "Okay, mom, I have to go!" If he only knew what the man on the phone had just told me and how I was feeling inside, he would have let me hug him just a little bit longer. After he left, I dropped to the floor in a sort of fetal position and cried my heart out to God, asking him," what am I going to do now?"

Over the weeks leading up to and after my scheduled bilateral mastectomy in December, I went through what most would call an emotional roller coaster. My masks changed often. On semi-good days some of these masks were bright and beautiful. On not-so-good days some were dark, lacking vibrance, carrying my pain, insecurities, fears, and true feelings on what happened or was happening to me. I went through a period of emotional numbness. Emotional numbness is something deeper than what a person sees on the surface. It can be an intrusive thought, lack of pleasure, being clinically depressed, unable to sleep, or a recurring sensation of being outside of your body looking in or feeling what is happening to you isn't real.

WALKING IN MY SIZE SEVENS: After the mastectomy, things didn't lighten up for me. Due to my other health issues, I didn't have the opportunity for them to make my breast using my own fat like my mom had done many years ago. However, I remember having an in-office conversation with the doctor where information was given, including a visual aid in the form of a 700cc H.P. implant. I ended up choosing the only other option besides going completely flat: to have tissue expanders (temporary empty implants gradually inflated with saline over time) put in immediately with weekly injections. This procedure stretches the skin and muscles if the expanders are placed under the muscles to make room for the breast implants. Unfortunately, my body didn't respond well to this procedure, and I suffered a lot. The amount of fluid being injected eventually decreased. Instead of weekly injections the doctor thought it was best to start bi-weekly to give my body some time to recover.

Eventually, it was time for the "big swap," as some of my fellow breasties (women diagnosed with breast cancer) call it. It is when the expanders are taken out, and implants are put in. Again, I was on a roller coaster through the emotional scale. After the "big swap," one would think everything would be great, but more pain emotionally and physically arose. Physically, I hurt so much that it felt like two big rocks stuck to my chest wall and then another cancer scare.

Proclaiming Wholeness Beyond The Blemishes Of Cancer

In 2015, I developed a 5 cm tumor on my left thyroid. Are you kidding me? What is it with the left side of my body? I was scheduled for surgery at once, and they removed the tumor and my left thyroid. Unfortunately, my bonus Dad (my brother's biological father who also helped raise me) passed that weekend. I won't ever call him my stepfather because he was so much more. To me, he was the man who stepped in, giving me guidance, love, and support.

Two months later, in November, I had another scare at work. We had a power outage that day, so I couldn't see any clients. My co-worker, with whom I shared an office, told me I didn't look well, and she thought I needed to be seen by a doctor. I drove myself about 20-25 minutes to the doctor's office. How I did it, I don't know; all I can say is BUT GOD! He sent his angels to protect me as I drove that far in so much pain. I went into the back and again fought another medical professional to listen to me, review my records, and basically HELP ME! My oldest son, my caregiver, ended up coming to pick me up and he said, "Mom, you have to call someone to help you." I ended up pressing the first number I saw under the doctor, and another one of my medical heroes answered and said, "knowing your history, this definitely doesn't sound like a stomach bug. You must go to the hospital; I will let Dr. Jones know the situation." Fast forward to a while later, I woke up in I.C.U. (pulled out my breathing tube) scared, not

There Is Beauty Beyond The Scars

knowing what had happened to me. I was later told I had an emergency procedure that my airways closed, and my children and family were told to prepare for me to die.

I went from this beautiful (not conceited) soul to literally watching my health and life det deteriorate right before my eyes.

I dealt with so much, physically, but also, spiritually, mentally and emotionally. I was a wreck. I cried every day, several times a day. I felt so alone, miserable, and unpretty. I was told all types of things that added to my emotional pain; "you're not a woman because you don't have any woman parts, you are dishonoring God for being so depressed, you should feel good that you overcame and give God all the praise, do you know how many women would kill for a free boob-job?" I felt God had abandoned me. Deuteronomy 31:6 (N.I.V.), says we can lean on God's promise to never leave us or forsake us, but I didn't feel that way. The Bible gives many examples of people feeling abandoned. Still, at this very moment, not to compare myself to Jesus, I felt completely abandoned. As it says in Matthew 27:46 (N.I.V.), It is only Jesus, hanging on a cross, with the sin of all the world upon him, whom God had, in fact, abandoned. And in his anguish, Jesus echoed David's wail, "My God, my God, why have you forsaken me?" I, too, echoed those same words.

My feelings were hurt, and yet again, I swept them underneath a rug with a large pile of hurt, the same hurt that had been accumulating my whole life. I put on a mask while I was dying on the inside. Because of the stigma, I didn't seek professional help. I had an amazing big sister and brother (Pastor and First Lady, that I've known since 2005), who prayed with me and for me (when I didn't have the strength to), I had my Boober-Mama (a woman diagnosed years ago that gives back and helps support young women who have been diagnosed with breast cancer in Hampton Roads Virginia) who took me to support group meetings and a few other angels God sent me, but at that time all I could see were the tornado-like storms that wouldn't go away. I remembered daily crying out to God, asking him why he continued sparing my life to allow me to experience so much hardship. I just didn't understand. But just as I heard him before, I eventually (God's timing, not Jackinah Denise's timing) heard him say, *"My Daughter, Be strong and courageous; do not be frightened or dismayed, for (I) the Lord God is with you wherever you go."* – Joshua 1:9 (N.I.V.)

THE TURNING POINT: *"Maturity is the ability to think, speak and act your feelings within the bounds of dignity. The measure of your maturity is how spiritual you become during the midst of your frustrations."* -**Samuel Ullman.**

I could continue telling you all the dark and dirty parts of 2014, 2015, 2016, 2017, 2018, 2019, 2020, 2021 and 2022 on how the storms of life and health kept raging. On how I was so afraid to be seen by a medical professional because every time I did, I was either being sent straight to the hospital (which it seemed like every six to eight weeks I was being hospitalized) or diagnosed with something else like; Gastroparesis (the medical term for delayed stomach emptying), colitis, GERD, or even when I faced leg amputation (twice) due to Cellulitis (a serious bacterial infection that attacked the metal put in my leg from the car accidents), Sepsis, Severe Acute Refractory Asthma, narrowing of the esophagus, which causes a whole lot of fear due to the seriousness of not being able to breathe and tiny veins with little access where central lines, pic lines and a port has to be placed in my neck, chest or upper arm. Yes, I know that's a mouthful, but just think about walking a mile in my shoes, my size sevens. In my transparency, I will choose to tell you even though these size sevens (the size of my feet) have walked and climbed many hills, valleys and the highest mountains, my faith (even when it was the size of a mustard seed), in God is what kept me. My big sister told me to daily repeat both Romans 3:5-6 (N.I.V.), *"Trust in the Lord with all your heart and lean not on your own understanding; in all your ways submit to him, and he will make your paths straight"* and Psalms 91:1-2 (N.I.V.), "Whoever dwells in the shelter of the Most High will rest in the shadow of the Almighty. I will say of the Lord, "He is my refuge and my fortress, my God, in whom I trust." I have always had a strong foundation, grandmothers (on all sides) were some praying women, Grandfather and many other family members were/are pastors who taught me to trust God and bring my burden to him for he truly cares. But, in this season of my life, I was in my "Job-Phase," wanting it "Jackinah Denise's way." Like Job, I indirectly demanded a full explanation from God right at that very minute, but what God wanted me to do was trust the process, trust his wisdom, character, and plan for and call on my life. No more calling this person or that person for advice.

> *Sometimes the strength within you is not a big fiery flame for all to see; it is just a tiny spark that whispers ever so softly, "You got this!" – (Unknown Author)*

So, I started doing some self-care for my mental, emotional, and spiritual well-being, including revisiting the "*pile of hurt*" underneath that enormous rug. I enrolled in a class facilitated by the counseling department at my church called "Forgive um Already." This class met for several weeks, and we worked out a book called *The Bait of Satan by John Bevere*. I spent more time developing my relationship with God and less on social media. Some studies show the roles social media plays in a person's life and how it has a direct link to depression and anxiety. I also had a heart-to-heart with my two sons, my biggest supporters, my caregivers, and my reasons to keep *fighting* for ME and *advocating*. Being a young mother with my own baggage and their only parent, I felt it was necessary to work on and continue building a healthy relationship with them to take steps in breaking the cycle. So, I waited and God sent the right person(s) to help me in my time of need. Isaiah 40:31 (N.I.V.), *"But they that wait upon the Lord shall renew their strength; they shall mount up with wings as eagles; they shall run, and not be weary, and they shall walk, and not faint."* I got a Life Coach, who helped me emotionally detox. And I did the unimaginable; sought the help of a professional. Yes, in our community of black and brown people, we are not very open to acknowledging psychological problems or seeking help from a licensed professional due to:

- *The huge stigma associated with mental illness. Many people have difficulty admitting that they need professional help because they don't want to be seen by others as weak or less than others.*

- *The fear of diagnosis and always being in therapy. No one wants to live out their life with a label on them that they believe will be permanent. What they don't realize is not all diagnoses are lifelong. A person can recover and live a healthy life.*

- ☀ *The fear of being judged by a stranger.* Even though therapists are human they are not emotionally involved. Instead, they are trained professionals to help you reach your ultimate healing by dealing with what is broken by giving tools to help you cope with your diagnosis and an outside perspective.

- ☀ *The fear of confronting the issue.* Denial is usually easier than acknowledgement of the actual problem. If you don't address the problem, you cannot find the solution which delays your healing.

WALKING INTO MY NEW NORMAL - THE "NEW ME": As one of my big brothers (someone I've known since 2002) has always said, "Sis, you are a phoenix!" But you have the choice to decide which phoenix you want to become, the dark phoenix holding onto the bitterness or the fierce phoenix rising from the ashes.

Today, I choose to become the fierce phoenix full of fire, light, and a lot of hope, forgiving myself and others while standing on the promises that God has given me to be healed, blessed, and a blessing to others. This time I am choosing the good version of F.E.A.R., Face Everything and Rise! What I've realized is even through my past and current storms, I not only have the power over what is going on in my life (including medical, family, and so-called friends), but I do have the power to change my reaction(s) on what is going on (storms, abandonment, unresolved issues, etc.). God is opening windows that if I'm not careful (meaning holding onto that pile of hurt, bitterness and unforgiveness) I will miss the blessing he has for me.

> *"We have different gifts, according to the grace given to each of us. If your gift is prophesying, then prophesy in accordance with your faith, if it is serving, then serve; if it is teaching, then teach; if it is to encourage, then give encouragement; if it is giving, then give generously; if it is to lead, do it diligently; if it is to show mercy, do it cheerfully." – Roman 12:6-8 (N.I.V.)*

No matter how many times I've run from my calling, I truly believe I was given this mountain to climb so others can not only see that it can be climbed, but so they can start climbing their own mountains. When we allow F.E.A.R. to set in, that is only the trick of the enemy trying to block and keep us from the blessing God has waiting for us at the top of that mountain. But if we only get to one peak or turn back, we will never receive the fullness of God.

This woman has fought a thousand battles and is still standing. Has cried a thousand tears and is still smiling. Has been broken, betrayed, abandoned, and rejected, *but* she still walks proudly, laughs loud, strives to live without fear, and loves without doubt. *This woman* is beautiful, strong, and humble. *This woman, she* isn't damaged, she is a *survivor perfectly imperfect*. *This woman is me,* Jackinah Denise, *"THE"* Strong Willed Survivor.

Note to Self (and anyone else going through this):

> *"Today is the opportunity to build the tomorrow you want." - Ken Poirot*

No longer will you allow fear and unforgiveness to keep you from fulfilling your God-given purpose. Heartbreak and deception are inevitable, but never allow them to change you negatively. *Learn from it, grow from it, and become a better version of yourself,* one that you can look in the mirror and be proud of. It doesn't matter if someone else doesn't see your worth, it doesn't diminish who you are as a person. God can take your brokenness and heal you while healing someone else who's watching you. When you learn how to *see the beauty beyond the scars* of cancer or any other chronic disease/illness or life-altering situations, you can begin walking in your purpose and seeing the fullness of God. You become *free* to *live* and *thrive* and not just *survive*.

When you realize you have the power to change your narrative by changing your mindset you heal your body, and to heal your body you must change your mindset.

You are kind, powerful, loved, valued, smart, and strong; *You are enough!* Remember, *Beyond the Scars you are a Strong Willed Survivor,* and you are loved.

SELF-CARE CHALLENGE:

Courtesy of Carenda-Deonne / Carmen Stockman

Take a 15–20-minute Detox Bath. You will need a bathtub, very warm water, two bottles of water (one to drink before getting in the tub and the other to drink while in the tub), towels, a candle, Epsom salt and lavender oil. The purpose of this Detox Bath is to release any disbelief, insecurities, and/or distrust within your heart, mind, or spirit. After soaking and releasing any stress, worry, fear, doubt, and unforgiveness, you want to spend 7-10 minutes speaking words of love, and healing. Then, rinse with a shower and relax. Afterwards, try to refrain from using any electronic devices for an hour.

*If you have pre-existing health conditions consult a medical professional before completing this detox bath.

Chapter Definitions for Medical Terms:

Gastroparesis: is the medical term for delayed stomach emptying. During digestion, the stomach must contract to empty itself of food and liquid. Normally, it contracts about three times a minute. This empties the stomach within 90-120 minutes after eating. (Cleveland Clinic)

Colitis: is an inflammatory reaction in the colon, often autoimmune or infectious.
Ulcerative Colitis: is a chronic, inflammatory bowel disease that causes inflammation in the digestive tract

GERD: is a digestive disease in which stomach acid or bile irritates the food pipe lining. This chronic disease occurs when stomach acid or bile flows into the food pipe and irritates the lining. Acid reflux and heartburn more than twice a week may indicate GERD.

Severe Acute Refractory Asthma: uncontrolled severe asthma. It is a debilitating condition, that does not respond well enough to standard therapy and has many distressing symptoms. Asthma exacerbations can happen without warning, be life-threatening, cause fear, and result in hospitalization and intubation.

Benign Esophageal Stricture: a narrowing of the esophagus (the tube from the mouth to the stomach). It causes swallowing difficulties.

Benign means not cancerous.

Sepsis: is a life-threatening complication of an infection. Sepsis occurs when chemicals released in the bloodstream to fight an infection trigger inflammation throughout the body.

Breast implant illness (B.I.I.) refers to a wide range of symptoms that can develop after breast reconstruction with implants. It's also sometimes referred to as autoimmune/inflammatory syndrome induced by adjuvants (A.S.I.A).

But after a life-changing breast cancer diagnosis, reconstruction with implants can help many women feel more like themselves again, so it must be discussed as an option.

BII can occur with any type of breast implant, including silicone gel-filled, saline-filled, smooth surface, textured surface, round, or teardrop-shaped. Symptoms often describe "brain fog", fatigue, anxiety and joint pain. These health problems are very concerning for those individuals experiencing them, especially after women having gone through breast cancer treatment have often already experienced these symptoms due to chemotherapy.

Proclaiming Wholeness Beyond The Blemishes Of Cancer

B.I.I. impacts each person differently. Breastcancer.org lists the symptoms as follows:

- *Joint and muscle pain*
- *chronic fatigue*
- *breathing problems*
- *Sleep disturbance*
- *Anxiety*
- *Rashes and skin problems*
- *Depression*
- *Hair loss*
- *Gastrointestinal problems*
- *Dry Mouth/Dry Eyes*
- *Headaches*
- *Memory and concentration problems*

WHAT MAKES YOU A STRONG WILLED SURVIVOR

Lauren Wingrove

Do you wear a bra on your head
Laced with sparkle and shine
Do you feel like a star
Dancing through a diamond sky
Bursting into flames
Bright and daring for all to see

Until the fire fades out
Falling too fast
On the way down
You lose your crown
Shutting your eyes
Before hitting the ground

Just as you think
This is the end
And tears start to shed
You softly land
In the comfort of your bed
all alone in your room

Proclaiming Wholeness Beyond The Blemishes Of Cancer

Do you wear a bra on your head
In front of a mirror that distorts the view
Of the reflection staring back at you breakthrough the glass
And step over the shards
Of the girl you once knew

I know it's hard
To embrace your scars
And love who you are
You're not alone
You'll make it through
Cancer does not define you

Do you wear a bra on your head
In a sisterhood of friends
Shining and glowing for all to see

Do you refuse to give up?
Do you keep pushing on?
That's what makes you a STRONG-WILLED SURVIVOR

This poem is not just for those who have lost their breast to this horrible disease, but for all who have ever heard those three devastating words, "YOU HAVE CANCER" fighting, surviving and thriving."

JOURNAL NOTES

CREATE YOUR OWN NOTE TO SELF

DISCLAIMER:

Glossary of words is provided at the end of chapters. However, we urge you to seek medical professional for advice and guidance on your specific condition

ABOUT THE AUTHORS

LAUREN WINGROVE

Lauren, a mother of one beautiful twelve year old daughter, Chloe. When she's not sipping on an iced coffee and writing she enjoys soaking up some sun on the beach and watching the butterflies. At the age of thirty two she was diagnosed with triple negative breast cancer. Even though her world was shaken she relied on her faith in God and her love for writing to get her though.

Contact Lauren at lauren.c.wingrove@gmail.com

MARY A.

Mary A. is from Greenwood SC, currently residing in the Washington DC area. Mary graduated from North Carolina Agricultural and Technical State University, is a member of Delta Sigma Theta Sorority Inc., and is on the executive boards of two non-profit organizations focused on assisting children in their educational pursuits. Mary is a proud daughter to Mary, and proud mommy to daughter Mary, a fifth-generation name that started with her great grandmother. At the age of 35, Mary heard the words no person ever wants to hear. "You have cancer." She found strength in her faith and in knowing she must raise her daughter. She referenced Psalms 27:13(KJV),

"¹³ I had fainted, unless I had believed to see the goodness of the LORD in the land of the living." Mary is excited to share her story of the power of believing in the possible.

Contact Mary at

<u>msmarymclean@gmail.com</u>

ERICA "LALA" MORGAN

Erica "Lala" Morgan, mother and grandmother of 8, and 7-year cancer survivor. Erica is very family oriented and enjoys spending time with them doing road trips, trampoline parks, cooking together and so much more. Since 2019 for her birthday and pre COVID, she wanted to do things that were different but encouraged her to live and enjoy life. So, in June of 2019 she went indoor skydiving, and it was an amazing feeling and scary at first. The next adventure for her will be zip lining. Cancer has taught Erica to experience life and the fullness of it. When she was diagnosed, her social club of ten years, Ladies of Zaki, Inc. was there to support and lift her up. They were an important part of her healing. She has received many accolades from different organizations for being a survivor. The Suffolk Beast Cancer Society, Inc. Erica and her social club were featured on their brochure. She has been honored by Sheeza Survivor, interviewed by the local newspaper, The Suffolk News Herald and The Suffolk Police department just to name a few. She is also a current board member for Strong Willed Survivor/Beyond the Scars and has been since 2016.

Contact Erica at

Va.notary4@gmail.com

There Is Beauty Beyond The Scars

LEONETTA JULES   TANEJA JULES

Leonetta Jules born November 1977 in Hampton Va is a wife and mother of 3 beautiful girls and 2 grandchildren. She is a cosmetologist by trade and a nursing assistant. She specializes in hair regrowth and restoration and hair loss solutions for alopecia sufferers with special care to

Those who are battling alopecia due to cancer related issues.

Taneja Jules born September 17 2004 graduates from Phoebus High School in 2022 and is currently pursuing a career in culinary arts. She is an advocate for anti bullying and loves to work with children especially those who have a history of being bullied or disability.

Proclaiming Wholeness Beyond The Blemishes Of Cancer

> Contact Leonetta & Taneja at
> wakeupmzjules@gmail.com

There Is Beauty Beyond The Scars

AMBER CURTIS

Her name is **Amber Curtis**, but the people who know her the best either call her Spork or Ambs. She grew up in Newport News, Virginia and was moved to western Virginia to live with her paternal grandmother at the age of 15- after her mother passed from cancer and her father kicked her out, because she didn't fit in with his new family. She's 22 now, and works full-time managing a dive bar in Williamsburg, Virginia, which means she also manages the lives, loves, thoughts, and day-to-day interactions of at least a hundred people a day. She didn't go to college, but she's well-educated in people, and how their minds work, as well as their hearts. She loves what she does, and hopes to one day own and operate her own place that so many people call their second home. When she isn't working, she is singing karaoke or spending time with her family and close friends. The cards have been stacked against her for a decent amount of her life, but not one time did she ever doubt she was going to make it, because she's her mother's daughter, and every storm runs out of rain.

Contact Amber at
Amber.brooke.curtiss@gmail.com

There Is Beauty Beyond The Scars

MICHELLE WICKER   JORDYNNE WICKER

Michelle Wicker was born and raised in Norfolk, VA. She graduated from Lake Taylor High School in 1996 and went on to graduate from Virginia Tech with a Bachelor of Science in Hospitality & Tourism Management. Michelle has made a career out of managing hotels for our US Navy. She has managed several hotels in Virginia, Texas, Japan and Washington state. She is currently living in Virginia Beach, VA.

Michelle enjoys reading, watching television, anything Virginia Tech and hanging out with her family. Michelle is the proud mother of Jordynne and their Japanese Kai-Ken (dog), Mazie.

Proclaiming Wholeness Beyond The Blemishes Of Cancer

JordynneWicker is 17 years old and currently wrapping up her senior year of high school. She plans to attend college and study special education, focusing on those with autism and minoring in sign language. She has a passion for volleyball but continues to play a variety of sports year-round. She has lived in a variety of places around the world including Japan, Texas, Washington state, and Virginia, where she was born and is currently residing.

Jordynne's schedule remains full with school, sports, work, baby-sitting and pet-sitting. She also serves as a Student Representative of the Norfolk School Board and as the President of her local National Honor Society and then as the Vice-President of KidzLink. In the spare time she manages to find, Jordynne loves to travel and is always willing to try new things.

Contact Michelle & Jordynne at

Vt17jordynne@yahoo.com

MELODY HANSLEY

Melody Hansley is a single mom, woman of a faith, best selling contributing author and Certified From Grief to Gratitude Empowerment Coach. Her passion for working with women began immediately after graduating High School, when she started working as a hairstylist. Melody opened her own hair salon called "Expressions Beauty Salon" where she welcomed women to enter in and fully express their emotions helping transform their outer appearance and inner feelings. From there, Melody went on to overcome her own life's obstacles, pursuing a degree in Social Science, and achieving a major milestone as she graduated from college walking the stage alongside her oldest daughter.

Melody is currently a Case Manager at the HER Shelter, a Women's Domestic Violence Shelter, in Portsmouth, VA., where she encourages women through her own personal experiences of Domestic Violence, narcissistic and psychological abuse. She has served on the NICU Family Advisory Board at CHKD (Children of the Kings Daughters) Hospital in Norfolk VA empowering other mothers who, like herself, endured premature births. Melody served two years as Parent Chair at Marriner Christian Academy in Portsmouth, VA. She is a Board member and blogger for She Steps Forward International Ministries, and served as Vice President for the Portsmouth (PTA) Parent and Teachers Association. Melody also is a member of The Tidewater Coalition For The People and serves on the board of the Peachtree Homeowners Association.

Melody is the Founder and CEO of M.O.R.E, LLC (Mothers Overcoming Real-life Experiences) where she engages women across the globe connecting them with other mothers to know they are more together and can overcome their challenges. Melody inspires mothers daily through a private Facebook support group and on the www.believeyouaremore.com website. She hosts an annual retreat for moms along with empowerment workshops.

Contact Melody at

www.believeyouaremore.com

JACKINAH DENISE

Jackinah Denise, affectionately known as "**THE" STRONG WILLED SURVIVOR**," is a native of Pittsburgh, Pennsylvania. Even though she has traveled and lived all around the world she definitely bleeds black and yellow, the colors of her hometown sports teams.

Our Strong Willed Survivor, is a child of God, a devoted mother of two sons: Jay (age twenty-seven) and Mike (age twenty), a proud big sister, a fun-loving aunt and a daughter of a coronary artery disease and cancer survivors. She is most known for saying, *"**Beyond the Scars I AM a STRONG WILLED SURVIVOR FIGHTING For Me And ADVOCATING For Others."***

At a young age, Jackinah Denise, knew her calling was being the voice for children and families. She has enjoyed her career being an advocate for our military service members, children of all ages, and now chronic illness survivors and butterfly families. In all that she does she strives to always wear her **C. A. P. (Confidence, Awareness, and Pride),** something she learned from one of her mentors Ms. Jean Bryant with the Miss. Black Teenage Beauty Pageant.

This amazing woman of **FAITH** has survived many health and life challenges; including being a young mother, divorced, being hit by an eighteen- wheeler truck, multiple surgeries and yes, she has heard the words "You Have cancer" more than once. But through it all her natural resilience helped her overcome those times of adversity and she stands tall as "THE" Strong Willed Survivor she is today. She has learned to "***See The Beauty Beyond The Scars.***"

Isaiah 49:11 "I will turn all my mountains into roads, and my highways will be raised up." Jackinah Denise knows without a shadow of doubt she was given these mountains to climb to show others God's Grace… God's Mercy… God's LOVE while climbing over those mountains and leaping over those hills.

Contact Jackinah at
strongwilledsurvivor@gmail.com

CPSIA information can be obtained
at www.ICGtesting.com
Printed in the USA
JSHW010850090423
40091JS00004B/52